Making Music

By David Keystone
and Cheryl Jakab

Contents

Sounds and Music

People can make sounds in many ways.
Some sounds that we make,
we call music.

The sounds of musical instruments
are made in different ways.

- The sounds of percussion instruments are made when the instrument is hit with something or when it hits against something.

- The sounds of wind instruments are made when air is blown through a tube.

- The sounds of stringed instruments are made when the strings are plucked or scraped.

Hearing Sounds

Sounds are vibrations in the air. Vibrations pass through the air from the thing making the sound to our ears.

Sensing Sounds

Make a sound sensor.

- Cut two pieces of wool about 25 cm long. Tie a piece of wool to each end of the coathanger.
- Wind the other end of the pieces of wool around the index finger of each hand.
- Put your index fingers in your ears.
- Swing the hook of the coathanger on to a hard surface and listen.

Junk Chimes

Chimes are tapped with a striker.
Make junk chimes from food cans.

Equipment

- empty cans of different sizes
- a hammer and a nail
- a piece of cord for each can
- a rod, such as a curtain rod
- strikers, such as wooden spoons, pencils, chopsticks

Procedure

1 Make a hole in the bottom of each can with a hammer and nail.

2 Thread a cord through the hole and tie a knot.

3 Tap with a striker. Listen to the sound each can makes.

4 Tie the cans to the rod in order from lowest to highest note.

5 Suspend the rod between two chairs.

6 To play the chimes, use either one striker or one in each hand.

Lagerphone

A lagerphone is an instrument that makes a jingling sound.

Equipment

- crown-seal metal bottle tops
- 40 mm nails with large flat heads
- a large nail
- a length of wood, such as a tomato stake
- a hammer

Procedure

1 Make a hole in the centre of each bottle top with the large nail.

2 Put the bottle tops in pairs, bottom edges facing each other.

3 Nail the pairs of bottle tops to the length of wood. Make sure they are loosely nailed.

4 Leave enough space on the piece of wood so you can hold it. Tie a piece of cloth or wrap some packing tape around the space.

5 Shake the lagerphone to make a jingling sound, tap it with a piece of wood, or bang it on the ground. If you bang it on the ground, glue a piece of rubber to the end or wrap some cloth around it to dampen the banging sound.

Plastic Bag Drum

A drum is a percussion instrument that makes sounds when it is hit with something.

Equipment

- large cylinder of tin, cardboard or plastic
- plastic supermarket or rubbish bag
- thick rubber bands, wide elastic, or wool
- scissors

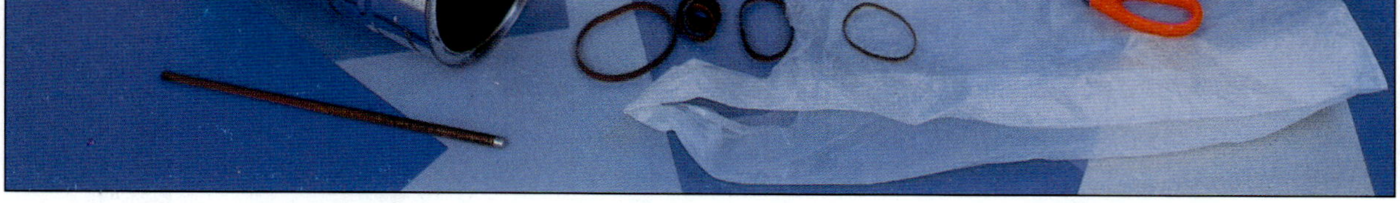

Procedure

1 Stretch the plastic bag over the cylinder making sure that you avoid any joins. This is called the *skin* of the drum.

2 Use a rubber band or piece of elastic or wool to hold the plastic in place.

3 Pull the plastic down from the sides so that it stretches tight.

4 Put another rubber band around the top edge, or rim, of the cylinder.

5 Continue stretching the plastic and adding rubber bands until the plastic skin stays tight.

6 Trim the ends of the plastic.

7 Hit the drum with your hand or with a striker, such as a chopstick.

8 Vary the amount you stretch the skin and listen to the sounds. Compare the sounds when the skin is made of plastic, paper, cloth and leather.

Straw Panpipes

Panpipes are a wind instrument. They make music when you blow into them. Make a set of panpipes from drinking straws.

Equipment

- 4 or more plastic drinking straws
- adhesive tape
- scissors

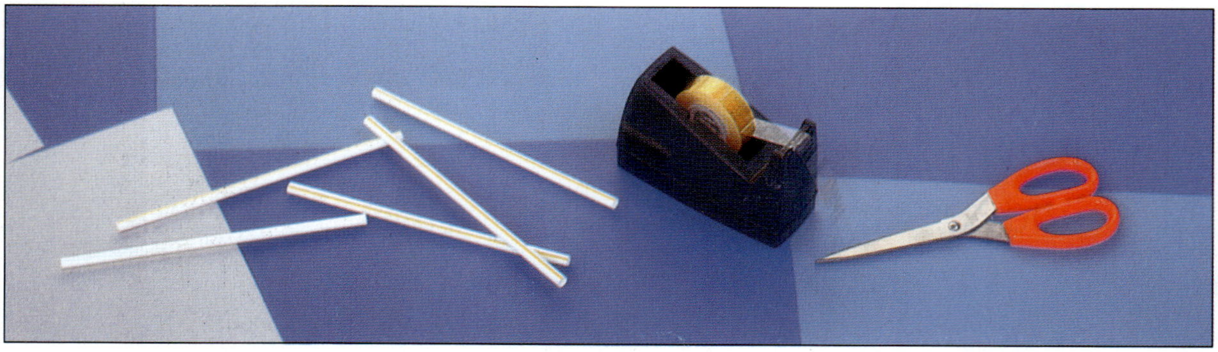

Procedure

1 Flatten about 2 cm of one end of a drinking straw.
2 With the scissors, cut off two corners of this end to make a v-shape.
3 Flatten the trimmed end with your front teeth.
4 Blow over the trimmed end to produce a musical sound. The sound will be quite soft.
5 Repeat for another three or more straws.
6 Cut the straws to different lengths.
7 Blow over the v-shaped end of each straw. Listen to the sound each one makes. Place them in order from the highest to the lowest note.

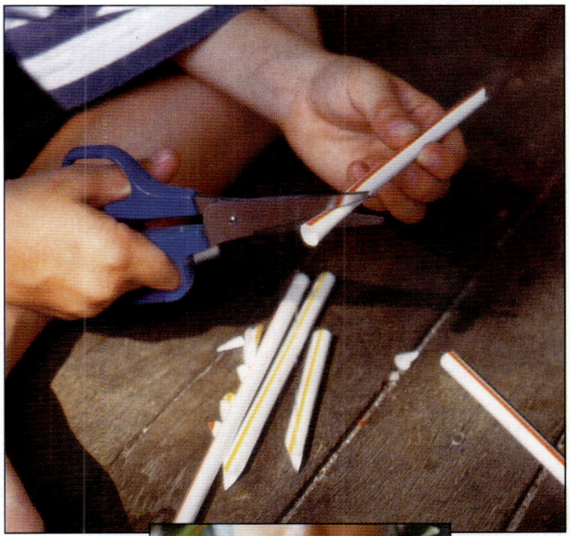

8 Bind them together with adhesive tape to make a set of panpipes.
9 Create a tune to play on the straw panpipes.

Ear Harp

A harp makes music when the strings are plucked.

Equipment

- piece of pine 20 mm thick and about 25 x 40 cm
- ruler
- pencil
- hammer
- 6-8 nails, 30-40 mm
- 6-8 screw eyes, about 10 mm
- strong fishing line

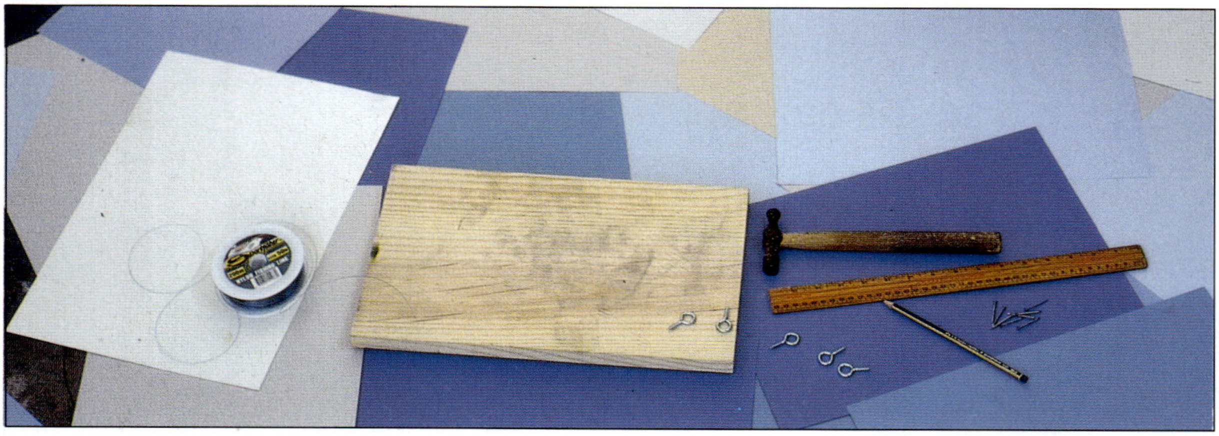

Procedure

1 Rule a line parallel to the short edge of the board.

2 Put marks along this line, equal spaces apart, for the nails.

3 Rule a line parallel to the long edge to about half way.

4 Rule from the end of this line to the bottom right-hand corner.

5 Put marks along this line for the screw eyes by putting your ruler at right angles from each of the nail marks.

6 Hammer the nails part-way into the wood.

7 Screw the screw eyes part-way into the wood.

8 Tie the fishing line from the nails to the screw eyes.

9 Tune the ear harp by turning the screw eyes. They are easiest to turn with a nail through the eye.

10 Play a tune on the ear harp. It sounds best if you hold it next to your ear.

Playing Together

Use the instruments you have made to accompany a song. Here is one idea. Sing to the tune of *Baa Baa Black Sheep*.

Key	drums	jingles	chimes	harps	pipes
					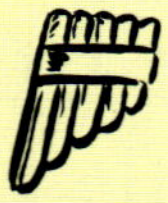

Bang bang rattle rattle

Shake shake ping

These are the instruments

That help us to sing.

Here is my . . . .

Here is my drum

Here is my . . . .

Now let's all have fun.

Now create your own accompanied song.

Around the World

Around the world there are many different musical instruments.

1

4

2

5

3

1 Australian Aboriginal instruments. 2 Bolivian band. 3 Home-made instruments. 4 Instrument modelled on an Indian sitar. 5 Scottish Highland drummers.

Index